THE UNITED STATES GOVERNMENT

SUPREME COURT

FRANCIE DOLAN

NorwoodHouse Press

Cataloging-in-Publication Data

Names: Dolan, Francie.
Title: Supreme Court / Francie Dolan.
Description: Buffalo, NY : Norwood House Press, 2027. | Series: The United States government | Includes glossary and index.
Identifiers: ISBN 9781978581616 (pbk.) | ISBN 9781978581623 (library bound) | ISBN 9781978581630 (ebook)
Subjects: LCSH: United States. Supreme Court--Juvenile literature. | Justice, Administration of--United States--Juvenile literature. | Courts--United States--Juvenile literature. | Constitutional law--United States--Juvenile literature.
Classification: LCC KF8742.D65 2027 | DDC 347.7326--dc23

Published in 2027 by
Norwood House Press
2544 Clinton Street
Buffalo, NY 14224

Designer: Rhea Magaro
Editor: Tricia Hoffman

Photo credits: Cover, p. 1 Sergey Kamshylin/Shutterstock.com; pp. 1, 6, 9, 16-19 Supreme Court of the United States; p. 5 VectorMine/Shutterstock.com; p. 7 Onur ERSIN/Shutterstock.com; p. 8 multitel/Shutterstock.com; p. 10 Carol M. Highsmith/Library of Congress; p. 11 Frame Stock Footage/Shutterstock.com; p. 12 Library of Congress; p. 13 Wikipedia; p. 14 Chinnapong/Shutterstock.com; p. 15 mark reinstein/Shutterstock.com; p. 21 Lloyd DeGrane/Wikipedia;

Printed in the United States of America

CPSIA compliance information: Batch #CSNHP27: For further information contact Norwood House Press at 1-800-237-9932.

TABLE OF CONTENTS

THE UNITED STATES GOVERNMENT

The United States **Constitution** tells how the nation's government is organized. There are three parts, or branches. They are the executive branch, legislative branch, and **judicial** branch.

The United States Supreme **Court** is part of the judicial branch.

BRANCHES OF GOVERNMENT

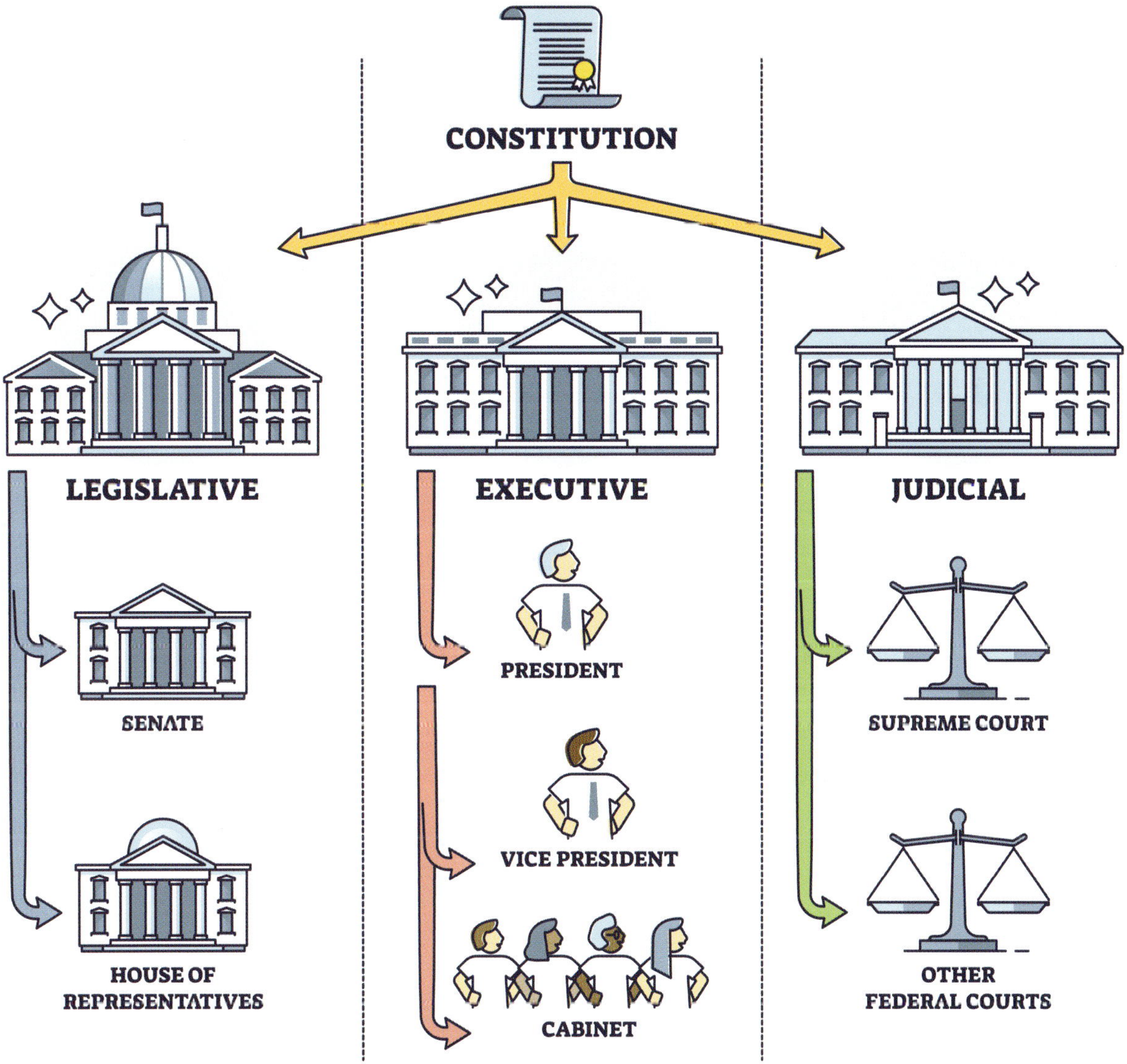

THE HIGHEST COURT IN THE LAND

The Supreme Court is the most powerful court in the nation. It has the final say about whether laws agree with the U.S. Constitution.

The Supreme Court can overturn laws. It can undo decisions made by lower courts. The other two branches of government must honor the Supreme Court's decisions.

The Supreme Court meets in the Supreme Court Building in Washington, D.C. It has offices for each Supreme Court **justice** and their **staff**.

The courtroom is in the center of the building. **Lawyers** come here to argue cases. The justices sit at a raised **bench** at the front of the courtroom. They listen to facts and make decisions.

SUPREME COURT DECISIONS

Supreme Court **rulings** are important. They affect many people's lives.

In the 1954 *Brown v. Board of Education* case, the court ruled that separate schools for white and Black students are not equal.

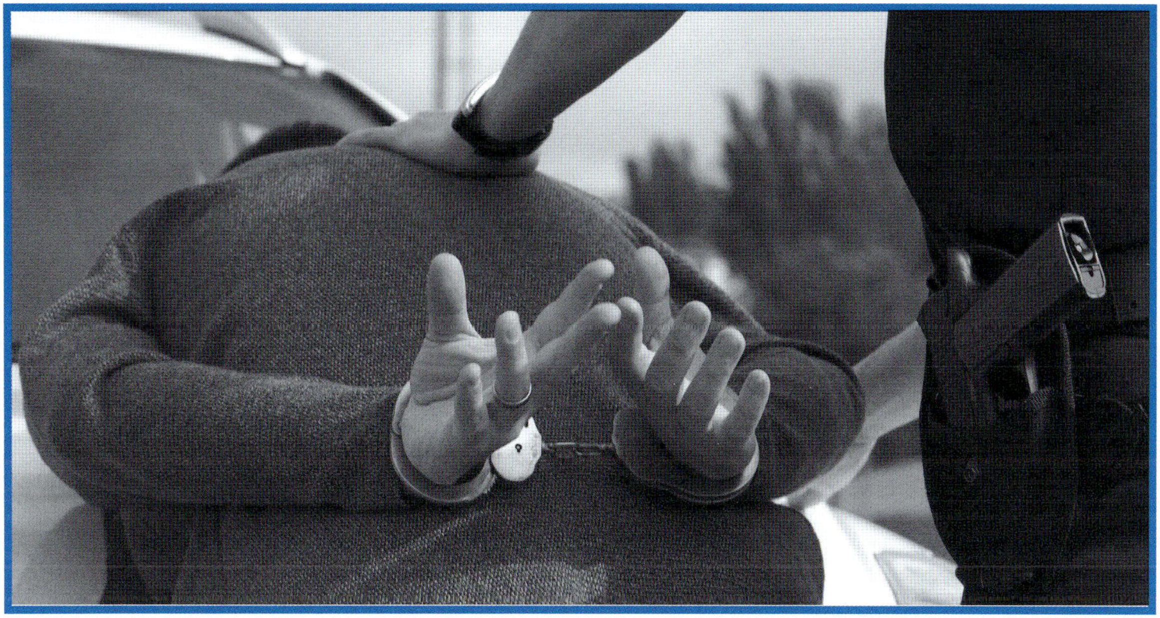

In the 1966 *Miranda v. Arizona* case, the court ruled that police must inform suspects of their rights.

In the 1988 *Hazelwood v. Kuhlmeier* case, the court ruled that principals can change what students write in school newspapers.

SUPREME COURT JUSTICES

The Supreme Court has nine judges, or justices. One of them is the chief justice. By tradition, justices wear black robes in court.

Each justice is appointed by a U.S. president and approved by the U.S. **Senate**. Justices can stay on the court for life. When one dies or retires, a new justice is chosen.

Supreme Court justices are former lawyers, judges, and college professors. They have studied the law for many years.

Justices serve longer than presidents and other elected officials. This helps make sure their decisions are not influenced by **politics**.

In 1967, Thurgood Marshall became the first Black Supreme Court justice.

Sandra Day O'Connor became the first woman on the Supreme Court in 1981.

In 2009, Sonia Sotomayor became the first Hispanic Supreme Court justice.

The current Supreme Court is led by Chief Justice John Roberts. President George W. Bush appointed him in 2005.

The nine Supreme Court justices today are (front row) Sonia Sotomayor, Clarence Thomas, John G. Roberts Jr., Samuel A. Alito Jr., and Elena Kagan; and (back row) Amy Coney Barrett, Neil M. Gorsuch, Brett M. Kavanaugh, and Ketanji Brown Jackson.

GOVERNING THE UNITED STATES

Supreme Court justices have important jobs. They decide if laws are fair, just, and good for the country.

What cases will the Supreme Court rule on this year? How could they affect you?

GLOSSARY

bench (bench): the place where judges sit in courts of law; judges ask lawyers to "approach the bench" to discuss issues in private during a trial

constitution (kahn-sti-TOO-shuhn): a document that sets forth the basic laws of a country and that outlines the rights of its people and the power of its government

court (kort): a place where legal cases are heard and decided

judicial (joo-DISH-uhl): related to judges and courts of law; the U.S. judicial system includes 94 district courts, 13 circuit courts, and the Supreme Court

justice (JUHS-tis): a judge

lawyers (LAW-yurz): people who have studied the law and who are trained to advise people and represent them in court

politics (PAH-li-tiks): people's individual beliefs about how the government should be run

rulings (ROO-lings): decisions made by people in authority

Senate (SEN-it): one of the two houses that make up the U.S. Congress; each state has two senators who help make laws for the country

staff (staf): a group of people who work to support an organization or institution

THINKING QUESTIONS

1. Which branch of the U.S. government includes the Supreme Court?
2. Why is the Supreme Court called "the highest court in the land"?
3. Where does the Supreme Court meet?
4. Give one example of a Supreme Court ruling.
5. Name one Supreme Court justice.

INDEX

ABOUT THE AUTHOR

Francie Dolan is a writer from Seattle, Washington. She is an American history buff who loves to learn about how her country works and how it has changed over time. She jumps at the chance to travel to Washington, D.C., and visit the capital's important buildings and monuments.